JUST POETRY TO MAKE YOUR DAY BETTER

SOME POETRY TO WHICH YOU CAN RELATE, SOME POEMS THAT MAKES YOU JOYFUL AND GREAT, POEMS OF VARIOUS THEMES, POEMS THAT ARE MORE THAN JUST WORDS THAN IT SEEMS...

RAJESWARY BEHERA

Made with ♥ on the Notion Press Platform
www.notionpress.com

I dedicate this book "Just poetry to make your Day Better" to my dear readers who are going through a rough day or a busy schedule and took a break for reading my poems. Sometimes words are enough to express one's feelings, sometimes a poem is enough make anyone cry, sometimes a poem can make one feel happy and safe. I hope you enjoy reading the poems!

The ocean in your heart represents the domain of emotions. To avoid becoming lost in this huge and complex world, one must

strike a balance between emotions and daily life.

Contents

Preface

I'm 17 years old, and I enjoy writing poetry because it allows me to communicate my ideas and emotions when I can't articulate them orally. A little poem can also be therapeutic; certain poems can captivate the reader and create an exciting, suspenseful mood. Certain poems can be compared to a beam of light in the shadows.

During my high school years, we had poems by William Wordsworth and Robert Frost. Their poems, "Daffodils" and "Stopping by Woods on a Snowy Evening," inspired me to begin composing poetry. I enjoy writing about various human emotions. I've written poetry in a variety of genres, and I plan to continue doing so in the future.

Acknowledgements

First and foremost, I would like to thank "Notion Press Publishers" for the opportunity to publish my book. Thank you for the excellent features that helped me finish this book. I'd like to thank my friends for being the first readers of my poem, pointing out where I went wrong with it and giving me useful suggestions for enhancing the poem, and encouraging me along my poetry journey. Last but not least, I'd like to thank my parents for believing in me and encouraging me to keep writing.

1. CHERRY BLOSSOM

This is a story of a man in his late twenties,

Throughout the spring season, each and every morning,

He roams along a avenue of sakura trees,

The light cool breeze rustles the leaves and the birds would be singing,

Some flowers of the cherry blossom were light pink, some white,

Some purely white throwing away a shade of light yellow in the broad daylight.

That man gazes at the sky and then at these flowers,

He gasps and utters in his mind, "She is like the spring sunshine."

He looks at the ground and recalls,

She has the beauty like those flowers and an everlasting vibrant smile.

Years ago he was considered a person with cold attitude,

But deep inside his heart was a kind gentleman just unable to express his emotions,

Women at his workplace would ignore him, talk behind him and spread rumours that he was rude,

He would talk about his interests, his want for true love and towards it loyalty and devotion,

The colleagues would say he was boring and pretend to have heard him,

He slowly grew distant from then, began finding his comfort zone.

Then entered a woman with a vibrant smile in his life,

Despite the rumours she heard about him she went to talk to him as he sat all alone,

He spoke to her comfortably, but feared if sharing his thoughts and opinions would be alright.

She would hear him out and was delighted with his company while others thought his heart was hard as stone,

She saw the mature and kinder side of his which drove her pain away as she shared with him,

The man heard a knock at the door of his heart which would open for her cause now he loves her,

He gifted her a necklace and apologised for it was not as expensive as those gifts she has dreamed,

For which she smiled and told him a quote, "Some gifts maybe huge, some are small, but the ones that come from heart are the best gifts of all."

He didn't know how to react but to admire her.

They both respected each other and love blossomed just like cherry blossom,

Today he was about propose her for marriage in the same avenue of cherry blossom flowers but she proposed him before he could say anything,

Among the cherry blossom trees as the pink flowers fell down, the cool breeze blew past their faces, the scenario was wholesome,

He smiled at her and hugged her dearly which made her feel more alive, a moment which felt everlasting,

Their love was as pure as those flowers fluttering in the breeze,

Their love sparkles like the wave of the seas,

Loving the lover more than the gift offered, talking without hesitation,

Being comfortable around whom you love, to cherish the person's attention,

It will of course take time for you to find your right person,

Just wait patiently you will definitely be loved by that someone.

2. CITY LIFE

The sky was blackish violet,

The city was calm and silent,

I sauntered past the streets all alone,

Only the street lights had brightly shone.

The leaves rustled in the breeze,

I stood among the dark trees,

That bordered the sparkling river,

Which under the night sky glittered like silver.

The fireflies lit up the dark surrounding,

This was the calmness I was longing,

For no wonder how many days,

This was the most beautiful place.

But now the sun will rise,

The busy city will come to life,

Again the commotion, cars honking,

People rushing to work and talking.

The sky is now bluish white,

The city was no more calm like that in night,

I walked past the crowded streets,

Where the morning and busy city meets.

3. SMILE

Hello, how are you doing?

I don't know if you're reading this to the end,

I don't want to bore you by asking how your life's going.

Just take a break now, my friend,

I don't know how to bring a smile to your face,

Think of the best memories in this difficult phase,

I think all feelings are important to express,

You can't say that happiness is the only good feeling that exists.

Sometimes it is good to cry all alone,

Turning off the notifications on your phone,

People cry, not because they aren't strong enough,

They cry because they were strong for too long,

Sometimes you may feel you are not worth enough,

You may feel no one understands you, but you're wrong,

Who can understand you better than yourself?

Now that you're still reading this, it makes me happy, even though I'm miles away,

Take a deep breath, relax, and tell yourself that it will be a fine day,

Well, making a day better lies in your hands always,

You can always chat to yourself or someone you trust when you're having terrible days,

You will resume your tedious schedule after this short break,

But you begin your work, perhaps without regret.

4. WHAT IS LOVE?

The sky was covered with dark clouds,

The raindrops cleaned Mother Earth,

Silvery raindrops made clattering sounds,

In the midst of the heavy rain somewhere in this corner of the earth,

A lotus flower was conversing with a rose on the heavenly ground.

The rose asked the lotus, "What is the true meaning of love?"

The lotus flower questioned the rose, "Why?"

Rose said, "Sometimes I am offered by a lover to its true love,

Sometimes I am offered when loved ones die.

But I see here different interpretations of the word".

With a smile, the lotus said, "Love is a complicated subject,

Love is not proven by just words rather by actions like respect,

Thousands of love-filled vows may eventually be proven worthless,

Such love has the potential to shatter anyone making them feel useless.

Saying "I love you" is a tough thing to say,

But after being said, for both lovers, it becomes a memorable day.

Rose chuckled, "But love can make one do crazy things like harm and destruction,

Love is almost like an obsession".

Lotus grinned and remarked , " Love is a word many like you misunderstand very often,

Different interpretations of the word like different seasons,

Love may change a person,

Or rather I would say, one may change for love in order to be accepted by someone".

*Rose questioned the lotus, "Why is a beautiful
flower like you happy in this mud?*

*Despite in this mud so dirty, grows thousand
vibrant buds",*

*Lotus retorted, "You only see the outer surface,
which is dirty but less,*

*The reason for my bloom is that water that lies
beneath the mud in excess,*

*Just like your red blooms make one forget that you
even have thorns,*

*People only see negativity in a person who has
thousands of positive characteristics to adorn".*

The sky was now clear blue,

The sunshine made the earth look new,

Rose realised and stated, "Love is a chance to embrace life again,"

The lotus was pleased with what it heard and slowly faded after the rain.

5. LIFE IS HARD?

Now don't think of your depressing life,

Just by reading the title above please,

I am not here to demotivate you or to tease,

Be grateful to your life why am I telling this?

The poor wishes if he a had a shelter even if it was small,

An unemployed for about 5 years now is still expecting for a call,

To everyone their probelms may seem huge compared to others,

*But why would one value their problems more than
their own life.*

If ever you feel left out just sit alone in a room,

Just sit in the dark or just close your eyes real soon,

Don't let anything into your head,

There is a reason behind your existence,

No matter if the situation is tense,

Never say no one loves you, it hurts,

*I don't know if you know me, just assume that I am
some stranger calming you down,*

You maybe pretending you're not in pain cause you all are experts.

There will be a situation even worse when no one will support you, that time don't frown,

Don't cry at your fate cause you have to make yourself one.

*Out of thousands there will be one to whom you
would pour out your thoughts,*

Learn to ignore all the negative taunts.

*Close your eyes and imagine that you're holding
God's hand and then cry and say whatever you feel,*

*Remove all the buried away thoughts bothering
you and the problems you have had to deal,*

*So before you take a major step always remind
yourself,*

*You need to be good and sensible to serve the good
people around you but again don't get
overwhelmed,*

THERE IS A REASON BEHIND YOU EXISTENCE THERE WILL ALWAYS BE,

DISCOVER YOURSELVES IS ALL I CAN SAY, HANDLE YOUR SITUATIONS SMARTLY...

6. SOCIAL MEDIA

She posted her pictures of her daily routine,

She spent most of the time on the screen, Cause in real life she felt unseen,

She was happy when others replied to her posts every time,

She felt relieved that she was cared by people even if it was online.

She had gained many followers,

The comments she received were better than receiving flowers,

But little did she know that among them were some stalkers,

Because she only saw the good side of internet,

Social media platform can be lovely and also an inescapable net.

But one fine day things changed all of a sudden,

Someone unknown misused her photos to have some fun,

Someone unknown used AI as their weapon,

All the unreal photos of her being bare in all of them were leaked,

The photos went so viral and her anxiety increased.

Everyone blamed her but it wasn't her fault at all,

The ones she thought would support her online were two sided after all,

"You wanted it to happen, you liar", "You are the reason for your downfall"

Everyone said this but not even one stood up to point out at the wrongdoer,

She cried in a video stating that she would never do that and her life was ruined just because that evildoer.

After that video a many of them sympathised,

But yet too a few of them criticized,

The betrayal of the internet community had left her traumatized,

She was just trying to make others lives better,

But what did she get in return? Trauma that she will remember forever.

What good does it do to one by causing trouble to others,

What if the next person targeted would be one of your sisters or brothers,

The wrongdoers, evil minded ones, the stalkers,

I Hope they get caught and repent for their wrongdoing,

And support the victim who is already suffering instead of falsely accusing.

7. THE SOCIETY I LIVE IN

I was born into a society,

Where people worship various deities,

*They fear the power of gods and goddesses and
praise their presence,*

But do not fear killing female infants.

I live in a society,

Where a woman is another woman's enemy,

They say a queen fixes another queen's crown,

But if you are a victim of abuse, then not all but some women would see you with disgust and frown.

I live in a society,

Where a man has no mercy on an infant or a woman in her nineties,

I must say that not all men here are bad,

Some are gentlemen, while some are the best dads.

I live in a society,

When a woman harasses a man, she is not considered guilty,

She then fakes that she was abused by the man instead,

Now it would be hard to believe the man's side of the story, even if he said.

I will be serving society,

*Where people first create problems and then solve
them, they will burn money,*

*A doctor's greatest reward must be the oath they
take to cure the wounded and ill,*

*But the same oath becomes painful when they have
to treat a rapist's wounds against their will.*

I am still living in a society,

*Where a well-mannered student, whether from a
village or city,*

Has to endure the hurtful taunts from relatives,

*But has least been praised for his or her
mannerisms and motives,*

No matter how good one is, if he or she is a victim
of abuse,

• 51 •

People will blame the blame the victim, and the
evil doer roams fearlessly without being on the
news.

I work so hard and put in so much effort,

To make even the slightest change to see a better earth,

I will still be living in this society,

With the hope that there is still a little bit of humanity,

I still wish to live in a better world,

In a society that's already sold, you have to love your life and treasure it more than gold.

8. RED FLAG

She says "He is a red flag but I am colour blind",

He says, " Doesn't matter if she is a red flag cause love is blind".

Being in a toxic relationship you forget who you are,

You're being used by your toxic partner.

You will still stay in that relationship because of outer beauty,

Even though you may disappear in the fog of toxicity.

If a red flag wants you then that person should change,

Why should you change to just to be trapped in a toxic cage?

All this may sound useless and boring,

Cause you are in the delusion that the red flag you crush on is well mannered and caring.

The personality of a person should attract before it's outer appearance,

Loving a red flag who can break your heart multiple times makes no sense.

There are huge trees bearing good fruits and then the rotten fruits fall down,

You see that the tree is so large to climb so you pick the rotten fruits even though you frown.

Patience is required when you find your soulmate,

Take your time to understand the behavior of the person you date,

Because at the end you just can't leave your love life to fate.

• 59 •

9. UNKNOWN

Four girls murdered brutally.

Isabelle, Amanda, Selena, Vanessa namely,

Killed on four different days,

So detective Selvan says,

Their hands and legs were tied,

Victims were tortured for hours then died.

The unknown killer was roaming free,

People suspected for the murder were three,

The first one Melissa Fitzgerald, an arrogant lady,

Who is said to be cunning and greedy.

The second suspect Liam Albrecht, a charismatic one,

Who is said to have murdered for fun,

The third Elisa Fredricks, who looked pretty outside,

But was described as wolf in a sheep's hide.

Elisa wanted to prove her innocence so she went through the case,

Determined to reveal the killer's face,

She heard someone behind her singing,

The same day she was found hanging from the cell's ceiling.

"Liam should be the murderer," Melissa suspected,

She found a code which revealed the killer of the dead,

Having read it, she started shivering,

Melissa heard someone behind her singing.

The code was:

"The first letter of the first victim - I

first 2 letters of the second victim - Am

*add first 3 letters of the third and first 3 letters of
the fourth victim - Selvan*

So you finally found me! Time to set you free."

10. LETTER

There was an old man,

Who walked by the lighted streets,

The celebrations for father's day began,

A child came to the man to greet.

He smiled and recalled his past,

A loving wife and caring son,

He smiled how things took turn very fast,

How memories vanished like the setting sun.

The very next morning,

The old man was found dead,

His eyes closed and still smiling,

He died waiting for someone, one said.

One woman found a letter on his hand,

She read it to the people around,

"Son will you not meet your mother,

I know you are always busy with your work,

Your mother is unwell,

She is always thinking about you,

We had to sell the place where we dwell,

A lot of difficulties we have gone through.

I know my death is near,

Please come back at least now,

Five years without you we had to suffer,

I hope this letter reaches you somehow."

He was a father,

Whose grave was at the lighted streets,

The celebrations of father's day was now over,

The same kid went to his grave to greet.

11. AWAY FROM HUMAN WORLD

All the good deeds you do,

Yet none will remember you,

Not every smile is real,

The darkest truth it can conceal.

The wind will wipe your tears away,

At your bad times when fake people betray,

A bitter truth you are ignoring.

A few may be caring but the rest pretending.

With a calm mind think twice,

Hatred was smile in disguise,

Far away from the human world, all alone,

In the end self- happiness is the ultimate goal.

A many will be sad seeing your happiness,

A many will be happy in your sadness,

This is a bitter truth untold,

I am far away from the human world.

12. FAME

Can someone tell me what's life?

Different answers I get alright ,

I have been thinking to write this song,

It's been in my mind for so long.

I hate to admit I enjoy this way of living,

Scenarios that I only keep dreaming.

They say why don't you understand us,

Why do you always have to create a fuss.

*But little do they know what's going on in my
brain,*

You have to just admit you're stuck in a survival
game.

Oh this fame is killing me deep inside,

To hide my tiredness I give off a fake smile outside,

Once you are pretty famous you know,

And when your fandom really starts to grow,

Your life is no more private from the others,

I just wanna have a me time where no one
interferes.

They say idol's life is the best,

We get money fame life is set, what else is left?

But wait, you're not wrong but I must tell you
something,

If you think we live like that you just know
nothing,

How could you forget we work under companies,

We rarely get to meet our families,

Oh then these stalkers get into my privacy,

So much insecurities that just makes me crazy.

But you know I love my fans,

They appreciate the way I look, sing and dance.

I know I am following my passion,

I don't regret the few giving true attention,

These nonstop concerts and hardcore steps,

Makes me feel day by day breathless.

Oh they pressurize me to go out of my zone,

I just wanna rest for sometime all alone.

But I got to entertain my fans even if I get hurt,

Ok that's it for today need to prepare for my next concert.

Note From The Author

Thank you very much for reading the poems. I hope you enjoyed reading, even if it was just one. If you've read all of my poetry, I appreciate your patience. You may have differing opinions about the structure or theme of a particular poem. My poetry express my perspectives on the world and how I interpret many things. I'll write another series of poetry. Until then, stay healthy, stay safe, and positive. Thank you; have a lovely and wonderful day!!!